For Connie
What a blessing you
are in my life!, Poetry
Loved!

Cheers,
Glenna

Febr 13, 2016

MATRIARCH

SELECTED POEMS

(1968-1992)

Glenna Luschei

The Smith ⊤ Brooklyn

Acknowledgments

We are grateful to the editors of the publications in which some of these poems first appeared: *Blue Mesa Review, Calapooya Collage, Caprice, Confrontation, The Decade Dance, Earth's Daughters, Gas, Greenfield Review, Interstate, Negative Capability, Oread, Prairie Schooner, Salt Creek Reader, Whole Notes.*

OTHER BOOKS BY GLENNA LUSCHEI:
Bare Root Seasons, Los Osos, Oblong Press, 1990; *Farewell to Winter,* Las Cruces, Dædalus Press, 1988; *Here,* Atascadero, Solo Press, 1989; *Silk & Barbed Wire,* Atascadero, Solo Press, 1986; *30 Songs of Dissolution,* Cerillos, San Marcos Press, 1977; and *Unexpected Grace,* Isla Vista, Turkey Press, 1984.

Published by The Smith
69 Joralemon Street, Brooklyn, NY 11201
Typography by Pineland Press
1074 Feylers Corner Road, Waldoboro, ME 04572

Library of Congress Cataloging-in-Publication Data:

Luschei, Glenna, 1934 —
Poetry
ISBN: 0-912292-98-9
                    92-080450 CIP
First Edition, July 1992

For the long line of Stevens women.

*And to small press pioneers,
especially Sidney Bernard and Alexandra Garrett;
and Ernest Tedlock, who first published many of these poems in*
30 Songs of Dissolution,
San Marcos Press, 1977.

*And thank you,
Karl Shapiro!*

Table of Contents

Introduction by Hugh Fox   ix

Moonstone Beach   15
Men with Their Secret Gardens   17
All the Time in the World   20
Injection   22
Bill of Lading   24
Matriarch   26
Eclipse   27
Wheat Straw   29
Jean Seberg   30
Secret   33
False Labor   35
Tenderfoot   37
Trailer   39
Divorcee   41
For the Women   42
Chevrolet   45
Class Poem from Prison   47
Flying into the Fire   50

Wing Walking   51

Race   53

Safe Deposit Box   57

How Will I Care for this Baby?   59

Rocking   61

The Blood Poem   62

Whiplash   63

Visitations   65

Mist   67

I Want to be Your Poet   68

Here   70

Arrangement   72

Roads to California   74

Wedding Dress   75

Sprang   78

Granary   79

Unnamed   80

Wise   82

This Rude Bridge   84

For Alexander Wat   85

Originals   87

Condor Rap   89

The Wrath of Sylvia Plath   91

Wait a Minute, Gloria   93

Introduction

First time readers, I think, are distracted by Luschei's "cover-up" personality that expresses itself in her poems sometimes as veneer. "For the Women," for example, a poem about sexual abuse as well as the brutal abuse of maternal instinct, begins with a kind of false flag: "I sang of the citrus./ I sang of the avocado and the lemon . . ." There is an inherent distrustfulness in some readers that shies away from female surfaces. Lemons and avocados lead them astray. But this "flag," this outer wall, is necessary too. Luschei is not a hatchet-carrier. She allows herself her full femininity . . . and sometimes even in the midst of blood, she finds solace. As in "False Labor," a beautiful poem about her delivering her own baby: "I cupped her head/ I eased her shoulders,/ ran my fingers down the blue umbilical/ bicycle chain . . . I cut the cord . . ."

The key here is in the next stanza: "Between then and now/ I sink in the marsh pond's dream." The marshy pond, in a sense, is a metaphor for all of Luschei's "compromising" years, living inside her full femininity and at the same time living in circumstances that grate against that fullness.

There are two lines in "For the Women" that both define the extent of her poetic territory and explain its boundaries: "I burn to sing for the women./ I was born to sing for the women."

In a way *Matriarch* reminds me of Helen Duberstein's *Changes*, a book not only about a woman's life from menarche to menopause, but how (and how differently from a man) a woman views the world.

Luschei's work is filled with blood-imagery, brutality, violence: "I remember the story of a goose./ Boys clubbed her goslings to death./ She flew to peck at the pulp."

In one poem especially, "Men With Their Secret Gardens," she confesses to a sense of herself as victim:

> *I carry a man on my coattails*
> *until he conquers me . . .*
> *There was always a man*
> *to unlock my cage,*
> *to throw away my papers, to enrage me.*
> *"Man the editor; woman the creator," I wrote.*

Take even what superficially seems like a love poem, "Secret." You can get led astray by the Rodin sculpture and the boats in the Bois de Boulogne . . . but that's not what the poem is about. The real subject is a primitive patriarchalism that disallows The Female any participation in the modern Torah-rituals such as existentialism: "Tell me," I said to him./ "about existentialism."// "Oh," he said, "you could/ never understand existentialism."

I like the daring of these two simultaneously coexisting levels, the unabashed softness of surrender to the feminine *and* the anger of the habitually psychologically-battered second-class citizen, "The thistle is as lovely to remember/ as the Chinese bell flower," ("Arrangement") counterpoised against "Gone// my yellow hair/ that sang to the trawlers." ("Wheat Straw").

Happily, Luschei never learned the trick of turning directness into cloudy, fake profundity, never was interested in time-worn poet roles. The genteel victimized nurturer, after all, is much more a human common denominator than the shock-artist, sorceress or iron avenger.

— Hugh Fox

"To my eye as well as my ear, American poetry is a relentless nonstop sermon on human autonomy; the song of the atom, if you will, defying the chain reaction. Its general tone is that of resilience and fortitude, of exacting the full look at the worst and not blinking. It certainly keeps its eyes wide open, not so much in wonderment, or poised for a revelation, as on the lookout for danger. It is short on consolation (the diversion of so much European poetry, especially Russian); rich and extremely lucid in detail; free of nostalgia for some Golden Age; big on hardihood and escape. If one looked for its motto, I would suggest Frost's line from "A Servant to Servants": 'The best way out is always through.'"

— JOSEPH BRODSKY

Moonstone Beach

O let me sing
with that American voice.
Let me sing
the song of the atom
at Moonstone Beach.

Look out for danger!
Only sand verbena
for a handhold
we slide down the cliff,
land feet first.

Bride and widow,
you wrote of such a white
and ghostly beach,
saw the moon cast
net upon the sand.
You were caught
for the rest of time.

Under the mushroom
moon
we search for quartz.

I'll wear the talisman
down
for luck.
The virus lurks here,
maybe death.

Let me sing
your song,
exact my full eye
at the worst,
that you may die before me.

I submit to the chain
reaction, the
shrug of the sea.
I voice the mantra of
matriarchs.
As long as we live
not one of ours will want.

Men with Their Secret Gardens

There is always a man
who brings me back from Santiago
When I have barely met Gabriela Mistral.
Even at the prison
there is a man who pushes open
the turnstile.

I carry a man on my coattails
until he conquers me,
undresses me,
saves me in distress.
A man will impregnate me
at the moment I am due to make a discovery.

My champions were men.
I bore sons. They drive me
to the homestead where I climbed
the apricot tree.

When I walk around the block
where I memorized the cracks
picked blue flax
they step on the gas. They honk

when I stop at the library where I checked out
Jo's Boys when I was ten.

Men.
There was always a man to
unlock my cage,

to throw away my papers, to enrage me.
"Man the editor; woman the creator," I wrote.
A man to shoe my horse
a man to operate the buzz saw while I dodge the splinters.
He'll fund my projects, give me money, take it from me
steal my daughters.

Men cover our fingers with secret
gardens of emeralds.
I wear the engagement rings of my grandmother
and three aunts. "Engaged."
Do you gain the trust of a heifer
to lead her to a distant place of slaughter?

One day I will take off all my rings
and give them to my grandsons,
never know who will wear sapphires for loyalty
rubies for heart
diamonds forever
only that the veins of my hands sprout potato tubers.
I will remember my happiest hours

(after men grow tired of uprooting me)
digging in my own garden.

All the Time in the World

My neighbor fears a killing frost.
I help her fill tomato bins.
Heat sponges our backs.
We pull green tomatoes from the vine
for making piccalilli.
The crooked neck squash blow up.
Up. We've got all the time in the world.

I planted my garden in Colombia
with seeds my mother sent from Iowa.
At night *campesinos* walked away with corn,
stalks and all.

I heard the city of sweet corn
ticking like a bomb.
In the morning children
came to our door with buckets for *avena*.
Our neighbor brought milk and I boiled it.

When squatters hooked into our power
the lines went down.
The electrocuted cattle

stayed three days in the meadow,
feet pointing up.

It's hard to sleep at night
among the vines that headline
Guatemala, San Salvador, Nicaragua.
Zucchini lurk like submarines
or caribe shark feeding
in the Caribbean.
All the time in the world.

Injection

In Bogotá where children slept on streets
under bullfight posters
three figures reach out of the dark.

The woman wears herringbone. She touches
my arm. "Señora,
Señora, this is my daughter, and her baby
is sick. Could you give us money?"

I am in my twenties.

I reason —
if I give her pesos
she may buy *aguardiente*.

I take her to the pharmacy
stark with light.
It smells of ether.
The druggist gives the baby an injection.

Years later, I wonder why I didn't ask their story.
Why were they in the street at dusk?

I had to buy meat for my family. I hurried
home to supper.

Bill of Lading

My passport has arrived.
It's time to move on.
I own my books and the dining room table.
My mother shipped it from Iowa
when they ran the highway
through our house.

Here I ladle Brunswick stew
I learned in North Carolina.
I publish books from this table,
elect the president.

One guest,
Camilo Torres, priest,
brought Marxist students to my house
the night before I left Bogotá.
Possessions stacked in cartons,
I listened for Colombian revolutions.
Waiters in black tie
served champagne.

One month later
I saw Camilo in *La Prensa*

dead
eyes still open.

I can't blame my table for what happened
in the Andes
for the highway through the plains.
Poets write.
Revolutions form.
Hear a baby cry every morning.

Matriarch

Remember when the oak crashed into the roof?
Branches longer than the house,
allowed the tree to topple.
That was the November Joseph died.

I tend the Dickenson, tallest avocado
in the orchard.
Head and shoulders above the rest,
it draws me back when I get lost.
We sell some fruit
but I preserve the tree for history.

My garden cultivates me, tears me
from my typewriter. Cymbidia shows its
first spike in January.

Remember when we pulled apart
those tangled veins beneath the oak?
That was the November Joseph died.

I make peace with my mistakes, admit
some things never mend, heal crooked.
I tend the orchard.

Eclipse

While the husband worked
she grew into her redwood house
as in her childhood story
of people who merged with oak
trees.

When she awoke to acorns
dropping on her redwood roof
she knew she would be initiated
into the rite of trees.
During the eclipse

she crept out and spied the tangled
red yarn in the moon.
Blood lines in the moon.
She ventured one foot into the tree bark.
It yielded and she entered the tree.

She slept there until she heard
her husband chopping wood.
She gave him a basket of red
yarn. He grew plump and one day said,
"This house no longer suits me."

When they moved on
her necklace caught on the pump handle.
The pearls scattered
under the redwood deck.

She wondered if the wagon would bring
her back one day; if the pearls
would have grown into mushrooms.

Wheat Straw

The tractors plowed me
under
the deep grey loam

with shards of pottery
and arrowheads.

Gone

my yellow hair
that sang to the trawlers.

Jean Seberg

Jean Seberg came from Iowa as I did.
I loved acting, gained the lead in *Our Miss Brooks,* as Sister
Margaret in *The Hasty Heart.*

Jean did better. Otto Preminger cast her in *The Lark.* She played
Bonjour Tristesse,
married her French lawyer in Trinity Lutheran Church.

Her husband introduced her to Romain Gary the novelist (Consul
General in Los Angeles). She loved Gary and bore his son.

Gary said:
> You have to understand the
> Midwest. She emerged from it
> intelligent, talented, beautiful,
> with the naiveté of a child.
> To me her goodwill is infuriating idealism.
> It made her defenseless.
> In the end it came between us.

I understand the Midwest and love with too much innocence.

Jean married Gary. While filming *Paint Your Wagon,* she fell in love with Clint Eastwood, later with Hakim Jamal, assassinated for betraying the Black Muslims.

Jean wrote to *Libération*:
>Hakim Jamal, cousin of Malcolm X,
>ex-user, convict; the most
>beautiful man who walked the earth;
>he's dead, my Jamal;
>eight slugs in the belly,
>seated in a rocking chair
>surrounded by family.
>You killed my Jamal.

Jean was pregnant. The F.B.I., the *L.A. Times* and *Newsweek* speculated about the father, rumored "Black activist from California."

Publicity threw her into labor.
A girl was born by Caesarean, named Nina
after Romain Gary's mother. The baby died three days later.

In Marshalltown, they left the coffin open. People could see that Nina was white.

Gary insisted: "I am the father."

At the Left Bank restaurant La Medina,
Jean met Algerian Ahmed Hasni.
She started her film, *The Legion Parachutes into Kolwesi.*

After a fight with Hasni, she threw herself onto the Metro tracks; was pulled to safety.

I prayed for Jean and for those who've pulled me from the tracks.

She wrote to her son:
>"Be good and forgive
>the mama who loves you."

Police found her body in a blanket in the back of her Renault on the Rue de Longchamps.

Jean was buried at Montparnasse.

Three months later Romain Gary sat at his desk
and put a bullet through his head.

He wrote:
>"No connection with Jean Seberg. Lovers of broken hearts
>are kindly asked to look elsewhere."

Secret

Of my first affair
in Paris
I remember
brown leaves falling
on a sculpture by Rodin
skylights in autumn.

Sunday
boats on the Bois de Boulogne.
Once someone paid our fare.
We were lovers and poor.

I arranged our room
with Italian pottery
and scarves from Liberty.
When he flew in from Spain,
he gave me a knife from Toledo.

I wondered how to tell
my best friend, Lucy.
But I kept it a secret.

He organized his books.
Heidegger
Sartre from the Sorbonne.

The first night
we invited Lucy to the Lido
to watch the dancers.

Lucy said,
"I feel sorry for the one
with small breasts."

We all rode home in
a taxi with an open roof.
Lucy made me keep the cork
from my first champagne.

I kept my love a secret.

One night he and I
gave a party.
Lucy thought
engagement.

"Tell me," I said to him,
"about existentialism."

"Oh," he said, "you could
never understand existentialism."

False Labor

My daughter and her lover
pick me up at JFK.
They've got it planned.
She and I share the bed.
He'll take the lumpy sofa.
She tells me we may see
a whistling swan
on the ride to New York City.
It's lights out early.

In jet lag sleeplessness
I wonder
how many times
my first born and I
have shared a bed
since the morning
I delivered her at home.

I'd called in.
The doctor said the labor
must be false.
I took my sewing back to bed.

My body took the lead.
The tidal wave convulsed me.

I cupped her head.
I eased her shoulders,
ran my fingers down the blue umbilical
bicycle chain.
I forced back plasma
she'd need to live
separately from me.

I cut the cord.

Between then and now
I sink in the marsh pond's dream.
We dress to board the train.
The swan whistles
through golden light.
I release a rook and a dove.

We are together. The waters
break.

Tenderfoot

When we lived in South America
I read to you from *Junior Girl Scout Handbook:*
Baden Powell,
Swiss chateau and monarch butterfly,
hikes through the wild
and the tenderfoot badge.

Because of kidnapping
you couldn't go out without a maid.
You dreamed you gathered kindling,
lit tinder
sang "Tell Me Why" around the fire.

Back home you joined Campfire,
picked out beads, chose an Indian name:
Merry Hearted Leader Who Is Generous.

I'd forgotten
how many beads the mother has to string.
We didn't have a maid now.
There were three younger ones.
I left you to your own beads, your own room.

Your loom fell under the bed
your beads down the hot-air chute
you grew further from me and the fire.
Your room grew worse
with dirty clothes and mice.
The narcissus you lost in October
took root in your socks
and bloomed.

You barred us from your room.
What is the purpose of the cocoon?
Must a butterfly eat her way through slime?
Here you are full spread,
luminous!
Your room is clean.

The story isn't over.
Your father and I each twists
a wing.
Which way will you turn in the divorce?

I feel you slip through my palms
feel pollen on my hands.
Will you fly back?
Can we be friends?
Merry Hearted Leader Who Is Generous.

Trailer

When you moved
into the trailer with your father
you charted a map
on four pieces of spiral paper
and with a magic marker traced
a purple trail,
glued it to my door.

Now

if there were a guerrilla shoot-out
and my house
went for headquarters
would their leader —
an expert on maps and hideouts —
reconnoiter
and know you were my daughter
and not consider
that you had moved away from me
but see instead
between every child of revolution
and her mother
there's a magic marker

a persistent and an often severed trail
through notebook holes
through stops and goes
past the shopping center.

Divorcee

Then it's the turn
of your attorney
to pick you off like a sitting duck.
Why do they say the divorcee
is promiscuous?
She's only a spruce
putting out cones in a drought.
Under threat of extinction
we all reproduce.

By this
we deduce the divorcee
is the guardian of wilderness
the priestess of swamp
and endangered species.
Don't confuse her tenderness with weakness.
She's a snow goose of many migrations.
Gentlemen of the courts,
take her gently
and with respect.

For the Women

1.

I sang of the citrus.
I sang of the avocado and the lemon.
It's time for me to sing of women.

The young woman with the straight
nose and the oval face — a beauty
stands up
to tell her story:

> My father abused me when I was 6 until
> I was 12. No one believed me. They
> believed my father, a corporate lawyer.

She speaks dry-eyed.
Water in my ears makes me hear
for the first time.

2.

After the meeting
my friend's hysterectomy:

All the people who gave me blood are
in my veins. It was a flood of love.
If I had known my daughter had chosen
my womb to learn from me
I would have treated her in a different
way. Last night the raccoons got our
mother duck. She never left the nest.
The message is not to get upset
with nature, to let it have its way.

I remember the story of a goose.
Boys clubbed her goslings to death.
She flew to peck at the pulp.

    I too have grieved dumb,
    dry-eyed.

3.

That night
I dream that Bill, my dad and I are looking
at houses.
We enter a giant kitchen.
Bill examines the fuses, shouts,
"The attic's on fire!"
He is reading my gauges.

My blaze was always controlled
always rose from the chimney.

During the affair with the lawyer
I was dry-eyed as an alligator.
I took care of the accidents, got people
to hospitals,
to college,
through divorce.

Now I'm burning up the house.

I burn to sing for the women.
I was born to sing for the women.

Chevrolet

"Let him keep
the encyclopedia."
— Lawrence Ferlinghetti

Though I'm driving around
with my clothes in the back
of my Chevrolet
and my blouses flap through the breeze
and one shoe is lost
and I'm getting divorced
one half of the soul is free.

It once was community property.
Yes, Dear, whatever you think
but now it's my own
and I can fly
flapping clothes in my Chevrolet.

Though he rips me off
when I glide out
and steals books A to Z,

45

if we're measured by what we can do without
my wingspan can only increase.
"Half of the soul
grows freer each day,"
sing the clothes in my Chevrolet.

Class Poem from Prison

I. GOING HOME

Whop! Whop! Whop! of the Huey's blades
sliced the humid air.
"Hear that, Sarge?" The words staggered
from Joe's lips. A glaring form
appeared.
Joe's mind whipped down
towards darkness.
Did he ever hear the medic's words?
"Grab a body bag. We're too late."

How sweet freedom is. It arrives
in the moment you least expect it.

I've shot men and held them as they die.
When you go to prison, everything changes.

Visiting room mural:
"Yes — my body is in prison
doing what it must as the servant of my time.
In spirit, I am free to go home."

How sweet freedom is. It arrives
in the moment you least expect it.

Ting's mural:
Art comes as a courier from far away.
We nourish art; it feeds us.

II. CYCLONE FENCES

I received the full thrust
of the Justice
sword
like the proctoscopic exams
I used to do.

I've shot men and held them as they die.
When you go to prison, everything changes.

My mother's second son
was to be named
Edward.
There was another of course,
Plantagenet.

My Anglophile brother told me
the Plantagenet screams were heard

outside the prison walls, sixteen
feet thick.

*"Yes — my body is in prison
doing what it must as the servant of my time.
In spirit, I am free to go home."*

There are no walls here, just
cyclone fences
topped with concertina wire.
Though I'm screaming,
no one hears.

When you go to prison, everything
changes.

Juan, Carlos, Jim, Dale and Glenna

Flying into the Fire

You are a veteran of four wars.
In Vietnam you turned to
your dead co-pilot
and saw the fear still on his face.

When you went home with the body,
his mother asked,
"Why wasn't it you instead?"

In Jerusalem a bomb
killed your wife
while she sat with you on the park bench.

Now I fly into the fire.
I have escaped death
too many times.

I will not rest until all the children
have enough to eat.

Wing Walking

Far below me, Sedona, Arizona:
red canyon 500 miles from the *Sangre de Cristo*.
I can spot Oak Creek Trail,
later the Colorado River, border
of the Golden State, spy the London
Bridge, silver thermometer. I take
my temperature.

Yes, depressed.
We begin our descent to LAX.
"Haze," the pilot announces. "Overcast."
Through the plain of wind machines
I enter the valley of robots.
Mercury rises to the boiling point.
I can't go to work.
I'm sick!

Turn this bird around. All roads
lead to Albuquerque
where sky empties the blue satchel.
Dash out to catch the elm leaf clatter,
alms for beggars of beauty!

The Sandias spit watermelon
seeds into the carmine evening.
The full Taurus moon sets off the alarm.
Break in!
Duende breaks in when death lurks near.
I'm there!

But I'm here. It's the instant of harvest.
I pick persimmons, oranges, avocados
at the ranch. There's a devil wind.
Firetrucks in the night. Santa Ana whines.
When will the *Migra* catch me? I'm illegal
in this country.

Race

1.

My United 747
lands on Nebraska tarmac.
I enter the history of flight
where my Uncle Wade
made news in his Jenny Crate.
He flew a Dr. Brewster to Kansas.
They marked the surgery
site with a sheet tied to the windmill.
Uncle Wade landed there.
All night he shooed cattle away
from the plane's banana oil.

We knew Amelia landed here
but did the Martians
in their saucer settle down
in the blowouts and sandhills?

Some say the Rainbird creates
those green circumferences.
We can speculate!

2.

Among farmers in bib
overalls and seed company caps
I search out my brother,
his wife, my nephews
and niece
back with her Rossin Ghibli
from the bicycle race.

At their home, the first priority
of peony and scented air:
the herb garden tour.
Sweet cicely, rue
that medieval courts used
to keep out plague,
tansy from the prairie.
Sheep's ear for bandages
to bind pioneers' wounds.

In my swoon, I'm the mummy
wrapped with folds of heat.
Cumulus collects upon me.
The air must change.
What will happen to our lives?

This moment holds forever
sweet cicely and then the rain.
It holds our race, I knotted

between my uncle and my niece.
Survive,
live today. All destinations flicker,
change.

3.

After rain we watch miracles:
comets and fireflies.
I fly with them
and tell my nephews
about Amelia, Uncle Wade,
and their great Algonquin grandmother
who journeyed from Virginia to Nebraska
in a prairie schooner

about my cousin Lillian and myself.
We ditched our bikes,
dated sailors in Long Beach.

About my own grandmother
who let me keep chickens in my room.
Once the mites got the eggs.
Inside we found the snaky
embryos. The shells were shattered crystal.

Grandmother and I searched out cucumbers,
spiky hedgehogs.

Runners of my children grow
from the mouths of my parents.
I harvest the word by which we survive.
Our legend races a long time.

Safe Deposit Box

In the vault I view the birth
and death certificates, finger
Grandmother's engagement ring,
cavity in the center where the diamond shone.
We picked an acre of iris and peony
every Decoration Day.
(I adored her spotted arms.)

And here's the pistol.
My forebears are buried in Furnas County
where Grandfather defended his brother
against murder charges.
Nebraska's first ballistic
test proved the bullet came
from Grandmother's pearl-handled revolver.

Uncle Ott got off. I've got one remaining bullet.

Grandmother was a great shot
and so was my mother in the days
of Bonnie and Clyde, but I'm the Wing
Walker, witness.

I spirit away the lore.
Family go on before.

My son asked me for the diamond for his wife.
My daughter-in-law with eyes
like smoking pistols
wears the stone that traveled across the
prairie,
that calmed me in the root cellar
during the tornado.

During those storms
Grandmother sang, taught me to spell.
She won her fifth-grade spelling prize:
the watercolor of Grace Darling.
Grace rowed out to her shipwrecked father.
She saved him from drowning.

I gave that painting to my daughter.

In my family, daughters save the men,
brothers defend the secret.
I lock up the lore.
Family go before.

How Will I Care for this Baby?

"Let me take the phone where the children can't hear."
Over long distance wire you told me:
     back room of the clinic
     dark for hours,
     tissue scraped from the womb,
     oyster
     from the shell.

     I sent flowers.

You called to tell your dream:
     a nightmare child
     grew so fast you couldn't hold her.
     How will I care for this baby?
     Who will protect this child?
Your therapist said,
"You will take charge of your own growth now.
You are the baby."

When I stayed in your house
I awoke to midnight shrieks.
A cat?

Coyote? Was it human? Was it you
keening for the baby, *La Llorona* of the legend?

Cortez stole his children
from Malinche
to send them to Spain.
She asked to say goodbye
led them to the river and with a machete
cut their throats.
The wind still howls across the canyon mouth:
      Who will protect my child?

You invade my home with the passion
of the gypsy moth.
All night I hear your pen
chew paper.
We are torn from the children by your pace:
to the train, to the restaurant,
to the beach.

The baby would be ten. I wish
she had been mine.

Rocking

The father takes the children
from the playground
I hear the giants clank,
an unbalanced teeter-totter.
I need myself on one end
my children on the other.

So many facets
to this baseball diamond.
In a visitation of silence
I hear the mesa creaking.
So many mothers
out listening for children
mothers rocking their babes.

Rocking chair, oh *mesadora*.
I rock myself to one side
my children on the other.

The Blood Poem

They told me about blood.
It didn't come red
but in dark clots of plum.
They told me about birth.
I would be twisted
from the thorax
like a box elder bug.

They told me that when a man
uses a woman
he will no longer be her friend.
Can't we live together in a golden ring
shining?

Whiplash

Just when I think I've arrived
I'm hit from behind by that black Peugeot
that some call fate
or Uranus.
Fool in the Tarot.

California and speed
mushrooms and mist of Dionysus.
Wherever I go the god of wine
binds me
makes me tardy
though drunk and inspired.

> *I do not choose disorder*
> *but relief from pain*
> *do not choose to dissolve old forms*
> *when the accident brings chaos.*

Some call it fate or Uranus.
Fool in the Tarot.
My neck rebounds
and the ambulance zooms
me back to New Mexico

where Zia dances
Kiva mantras
drive madness into rhythm.

Through ritual we mend
but lose chaos.

Fate and the black Peugeot
hit me again
drive me insane.
I'm back to the protean 101
of redwood and rot and madroña.

Visitations

The probation officer saved the
hardest question until last:
"Do men slide through
your bedroom door?"

Oh, there's a ghost
who slides through our shutter
creaks open our pane.

If you're watching these visitations
at my bedroom door,
Sir,
follow the fog.
It rises with herons
over the lake.
Catch a ladder of legs
and drift to rookeries
where the poor in heart can rest.

Jesus said,
"Take care of my sleep."
During the day if I feed each one
and don't refuse the bleating

for help
aren't my nights my own?
I own my sliding glass pain
and the ghost and the men.

We drift
to each other at night:
"Let me love you while we're still alive."
I've dressed myself in fog and wool
to tell you we are joined.

Mist

Once she saw him waiting
in the raw spring mist.
She unlocked the door.
She quit being late
to keep him from waiting in the fog.

He observes their rapid gust of days.
Mornings she drinks white sage tea
beneath the loquat.
He would bring her Red Zinger.

She would bring him the first Bing
cherries from Oregon,
a cornucopia of *cherimoya*,
but he is forbidden fruit.

Once she saw him at the door
in the raw spring mist.
How much longer can she wait?
He walks her past the sweat lodge to the gate.

I Want to be Your Poet

I want to be the poet
who invites you up the sweet-
smelling stairs.
My redwood home
would welcome the traveler,
sun on pine needles,
light through clerestories.

I want to be the poet
who sits through the night with you
cricket calling
cough of the kit fox
rasp of the newborn word.

I want to be the poet
who will weep with you
when it's time to leave,
who remembers
the burgundy of flowering plum.
Flap, flap.
Blue jay in the birdbath.

I want to be the poet
who can kiss you awake.

I'm not afraid of garlic breath.
I'll deliver CPR.
From your garden I'll pull out the onion
with a head like Einstein.
Get ready for surprise!

I'll whisk you through
the silk & barbed wire.
I want to be your poet, to be your lover.

Here

Love's in the daily doings
the blister on the first roasting chili
the race to gather sheets
at the wick of lightning.

We fold the linen with lavender
and sage.

Love's the oar that draws us to the sea.

You propel me over quick
silver waves to San Luis Obispo,
through spidery hills of black oak,
call me home.

The mica I bring you
scatters in my pocket,
but the hunter's moon
tracks it to the tarmac.

Why scan the moon's two continents for love?

Our friends shout, "Look around!"

It's here beside us
on the dark side.

We fold the linen with lavender
and sage.

Arrangement

It's 110 in Atascadero
with oleander in full bloom
but poisonous.

How could I change the arrangement
of this bouquet?
It's perfect
but I can't find the theme.
The thistle is as lovely to remember
as the Chinese bell flower.

When I bring together
silk & barbed wire
ferns curl about my fingers.
I haven't a green thumb
but I get by.

In Colombia
we gave away orchids
every day.
The boy who sold us cheese
round and moist as the Colombian sun
and wrapped in a banana leaf

asked me for flowers in a jar.
"I have to bury my brother,
drowned in the arroyo."

I like it here.
I belong.
I pass the snapdragons, stop
to give them water.

Roads to California

My dream sets anchor in your arms.
I water-ski
behind the moon
skim the Missouri where I waded
as a child.

Though floods whirled up to our back screen,
we children
slept buried in sand.
The gooseneck lamp
ran
with the ostrich.

Grain bins blew apart.
The highway swelled
with rotting wheat.

From Ventura you wave
cross the berm from creek to lemon trees.
I wake in the crescent
of your flank

I first knew the ocean at thirteen.

Wedding Dress

We take my dress
with wine stains to the cleaners.
Like pallbearers
we lay it out
up and down the counter
examine seed pearls
that "solvent will liquefy."

For no reason
I remember the coffins
my grandfather in Nebraska
took us to inspect:
They all had frilly white pillows
or peach, or leather.
"This one will keep your loved
one safe ten years."

Then what, I wondered?
Now what thoughts for a wedding!
My daughter will be married
in that dress.

I was a child:
The father of my friend
owned the slaughterhouse.
I showed up at 7 a.m.
to watch them butcher.
They shot a steer
in the head, washed blood
down the drain.
Sun streamed through east windows.

Still thinking about the wedding.

Barefoot,
I played in the lath houses
my father built.
Grownups strolled
home from evening
church.
I peeped out.

I didn't want a grownup's house.
I wanted a frame
where fireflies would swing
in and out.

Always I'd
lie on a warm night
on the banks of the Niobrara
ride my horse through timothy.

Wedding dress:
narrow shoulders,
a bosom like the
nose of an opossum.

Brave
coy
joyful girl with slender
waist, I became the matriarch
from lessons I was meant to learn.

Sprang

I walked out of the prison.
Before the gate clanged
the warden remarked,
"In the Grand Canyon
the rattlesnakes are colored pink
and mauve."

I worked in the desert so long
I envisioned the guards
were no more than saguaro.

No cactus could bleed me.

My antenna snapped.
I didn't hear the viper.

It sprang.

My students said,
"Take a bath in lye.
Grow a tougher hide.
Don't say goodbye. Leave us
with the magic."

Granary

At the Boston granary cemetery
the slate tombstones
with their primitive angels
and the skulls with wings
reside in beds.

Paul Revere lies here,
victims of the Boston massacre.

The placard reads:
This arrangement bears
little resemblance to what lies beneath.

I refuse to think
what lies beneath the New England soil!

The wind is low.
We buy scarves
and black gloves trimmed with fur.

Unnamed

My name is not known
but to the pear tree
on Lexington

the forsythia
whipping the park,
the starlings
that sing me awake
while the shark moon
bottoms out
with the lamps.

My name will be known
in the potter's field
where unnamed children
are carried down the ramp.
Prisoners bury them
50 cents an hour.

The sign above the cemetery
at Hart Island
reads:

Don't cry for us.
We are at peace.

Wise

You gave me
the fluorite cube for under my pillow
and the dream book.
The first dream: the gold mine.
The second dream: the coal mine.

With a lantern
on my head
I led the miners
down the corridor.

We could see the black
boots of the guards
through the gates.

Careful!

Evil's below.
On top,
the honeycomb universe
the envious clone, merciless drone.

You said, "Like the dove,
you baffle anger."
To become wise as the serpent
I penetrate the earth.

This Rude Bridge

"They came 3,000 miles and died."
I came 3,000 miles
jolted back to life by the minute
by these militia men
my ancestors.
in their tricorn hats
by this flood which arches in March.

Barley fields
fill
with water.
Redcoats practice with their muskets.
The re-enactment
always turns out the same.

My life — one chance — I signed
my name.
It's not over,
I won't give up without a fight.

For Alexander Wat

Alexander Wat, futurist,
jotted his lines the way a snake curled
in a jar would write.

I dissipate my poems like smoke
from a machine stalled dead
center.

Let me write
like the hooves of the galloping
Arabian.

You were in prison
when you had that vision of Satan
with hooves.
I have been stampeded.

You embraced Communism.
I, distraction.

You heard anti-aircraft fire
as the Devil's laughter.

I see waste.
Chips of my life fly out of the hopper.

I return each year to Nebraska.
You return to Poland.
Who can say that hell
comes only from bodily torture?
I, too, study
the nature of evil.

Originals

Karl, we can't believe it now,
but I used to be
your secretary. When *Howl*

came out you sent congratulations
to Ginsberg.
I took your calm

dictation in my impeccable
Gregg shorthand
then hied the letter home

for my army clerk husband
to type. I presented the originals
& carbons to you at 9:00 a.m.
clean as a new baby. You said "Ahem.
Good work." You, handsome
with your white hair, a real poet!

Luckily
I soon had a new baby. You sent me
congratulations.

When I came back you had a real
secretary. You looked guilty.
I cried. You said,

"Howl will change our lives."

Condor Rap

The condor's wings burgeon
beneath my trapezia.
Muscles flex.

Get out.

Fly over the Andes. Fly over sandy
Antofagasta.

O condor,

you're a tough baby.
Lady,
when you faced extinction
you flew back
and grabbed what you needed.

Lady,
you're crazy
if you don't follow your breeding.
Aim for the throat.
You're not the Amazonian
Pecho Puñalado,

caged bird with the wounded
heart.

You're grander than the American
bald eagle.
Admit you love carrion.

Admit

though life is a good chain,
life is a food chain
and everyone wants what you've got.

Everyone wants what you've got,
Old Bird.
The next time they circle
it may be over your delicate
bones.

Burst out, condor. Don't look
back.

The Wrath of Sylvia Plath

Sylvia, let me speak frankly
to you, angry
and red.
You died
on my birthday.
I inherit from you.

Let me speak frankly.
Why are you dead?
Why does the yew
reaching its hook,
mouth
of the dead,
penetrate you?

Sylvia, your children
needed you!
What did you think
when you left out the milk
and turned on the gas?

It might escape
from under the door,
poison them too.

Sylvia. I'm not through.
You thought you'd be saved
once more from the grave.
You had the call.
You'd return
from the chill oven's
lover breath.
You were saved
from under the porch.
You called yourself Lady
Lazarus.

Sylvia, I have the call
living against the odds,
hunger and cold,
betrayal and rape.
Your sisters do.

We needed your
matriarch's voice
as well as the tone
of the girl.
Sylvia, we needed you!

Wait a Minute, Gloria

Gloria Steinem worked years
on her self-
esteem book.
Her editor read it,
said,
"Gloria, you left out yourself."
She left out the child
abandoned by the father.

Gloria served her mother
bologna sandwiches in bed.
At ten
she wore her hair
to hide her face,
at thirty said, "I can't breed
in captivity," and "The examined
life is not worth living."
At forty
she slept in a loft,
crammed her rooms
with cartons/ paper/ books
for publishing her magazine.

She lived her real
life in airports.

Wait a minute, Gloria,
your life is beginning
to sound like mine:
boxes/ papers/ airports.
I did breed
in captivity
and raised my young
like the quail
who flies from her nest
to deflect the male.

I do examine my life
and blame the scatter.
I am not matter
but wind,
windmill and
chaser of windmills.

Gloria, you
put yourself back into
Revolution.
You fly
from one group to another
because we're the only
mothers we have.

Help me put my back
into *Matriarch.*
As mother/sister to my reader,
get us out by going through.

I embrace the child drowned
in the storm,
embrace my own, first-born.
The worm flew at her
on wind. I must keep her
warm.
"O Rose, thou art sick!"
I fear she will die
before me and Gloria.
I bleed in captivity,
in the wild.

About the Author

Glenna Luschei's first book, *Carta al Norte* was published by Papel Sobrante, Medellín, Colombia in 1967. Twenty-two years later she found herself teaching students from Medellín as poet-in-residence at California Men's Colony, San Luis Obispo. During the intervening years she has also been active in the small press community. Her journal, *Café Solo,* is now celebrating its twenty-fifth year. She has served as Chair of COSMEP and also has acted as literature panelist of the NEA. At present she is an avocado rancher. She is the author of a dozen books, chapbooks, and special editions. Her artist's books as well as those of her students have been exhibited at San Francisco State, University of California – Riverside, and many other universities. She has won the YM–YWHA Poetry Discovery Award and has been awarded both the D.H. Lawrence and Wurlitzer Fellowships in Taos, New Mexico, as well as a National Endowment writer's grant.